DANGEROUS

...OR NOT?

VULTURES

AND OTHER BIRDS

TRACIE SANTOS

Rourke
Educational Media

A Division of
Carson
Dellosa
Education

Before Reading: *Building Background Knowledge and Vocabulary*

Building background knowledge can help children process new information and build upon what they already know. Before reading a book, it is important to tap into what children already know about the topic. This will help them develop their vocabulary and increase their reading comprehension.

Questions and Activities to Build Background Knowledge:

1. Look at the front cover of the book and read the title. What do you think this book will be about?
2. What do you already know about this topic?
3. Take a book walk and skim the pages. Look at the table of contents, photographs, captions, and bold words. Did these text features give you any information or predictions about what you will read in this book?

Vocabulary: *Vocabulary Is Key to Reading Comprehension*

Use the following directions to prompt a conversation about each word.

- Read the vocabulary words.
- What comes to mind when you see each word?
- What do you think each word means?

Vocabulary Words:
- *defensive*
- *prey*
- *invasive species*
- *scavengers*
- *pests*
- *talons*

During Reading: *Reading for Meaning and Understanding*

To achieve deep comprehension of a book, children are encouraged to use close reading strategies. During reading, it is important to have children stop and make connections. These connections result in deeper analysis and understanding of a book.

 Close Reading a Text

During reading, have children stop and talk about the following:

- Any confusing parts
- Any unknown words
- Text to text, text to self, text to world connections
- The main idea in each chapter or heading

Encourage children to use context clues to determine the meaning of any unknown words. These strategies will help children learn to analyze the text more thoroughly as they read.

When you are finished reading this book, turn to the next-to-last page for **After Reading Questions** and an **Activity**.

TABLE OF CONTENTS

WHAT MAKES A BIRD DANGEROUS?

What do you imagine when you think of dangerous birds? You might think of sharp beaks or huge claws. The facts may surprise you.

5

Some birds are dangerous because they can hurt people or animals. Other birds are **invasive species**.

 invasive species (in-VAY-siv SPEE-sheez): a type of living thing that is brought into an environment and takes it over, causing harm

SHARP BEAKS AND GIANT CLAWS

Great horned owls have sharp beaks and **talons**. They live in both forests and open areas. They hunt and fly at night and sleep during the day.

 talons (TAL-uhnz): sharp claws of a bird such as an eagle, hawk, or falcon

Great horned owls will become **defensive** to protect their young. They will attack humans who get too close. They hunt and eat many animals, including cats and dogs.

defensive (di-FEN-siv): protective of oneself or others

Horned Birds

Great horned owls are named for the feathers on their heads. The feathers look like horns pointing up.

LOW   HIGH

DANGER METER

Crowned eagles are
the most powerful eagles in
Africa. Crowned eagles can kill
prey more than four times their size.
But they have not attacked humans.

 prey (pray): an animal that is hunted by
another animal for food

LOW HIGH

DANGER METER

13

Cassowaries cannot fly, but they can run very fast. They kill by using a giant claw on their foot to slash. They avoid people, but they have hurt and killed humans and dogs.

Dangerous Feet

Cassowaries have three toes. Each toe has a claw at the end. The biggest claw can grow up to 5 inches (about 12.7 centimeters) long.

LOW   HIGH

DANGER METER

15

European starlings eat the food that other birds need. They can take over the nests of other birds. They can make it difficult for other birds to survive.

LOW   HIGH

DANGER METER

17

Crows are common birds. Scientists think they are very intelligent animals. They have been seen using tools and solving puzzles.

Crows can destroy crops. Crows can remember the faces of people who have hurt them! They have attacked people and animals.

LOW   HIGH
DANGER METER

SHY AND SMELLY

Barn owls scare some people because they can turn their heads around backward. But barn owls are shy. They eat mice and other **pests** and have never attacked a person.

LOW   HIGH

DANGER METER

 **pests** (pests): insects or other animals that destroy or damage crops, food, or livestock

Turkey vultures are usually seen around dead animals. Their droppings can kill plants. Some people are scared by their strange beaks and bald heads.

But turkey vultures are **scavengers**. They only eat dead animals. They do not attack animals or humans. They usually hide when threatened.

⚠️ **scavengers** (SCAV-uhnj-urz): animals that eat dead plant or animal material or trash

A Gross Response

Turkey vultures will vomit when they are scared. The vomit smells very bad.

LOW HIGH

DANGER METER

Think about the birds around you. How are they like the animals in this book? How are they different? What do you think: Are they dangerous...or not?

LOW   HIGH
DANGER METER

LOW   HIGH
DANGER METER

LOW HIGH
DANGER METER

LOW HIGH
DANGER METER

MEMORY GAME

Look at the pictures. What do you remember reading on the pages where each image appeared?

INDEX

AFTER READING QUESTIONS

1. What makes European starlings dangerous?
2. How do turkey vultures protect themselves?
3. How do cassowaries attack?
4. Why do scientists think that crows are intelligent?
5. How are barn owls and great horned owls different?

ACTIVITY

Imagine you are a safety manager for a bird rescue organization. Choose one of the birds from this book and plan a building for it. The building must keep the birds inside and keep the people working there safe. Research the bird you chose. How dangerous is it? Make a list of rules for the building to make sure no one gets hurt.

ABOUT THE AUTHOR

Tracie Santos loves learning and writing about animals. She has worked in zoos and aquariums with some of the world's most dangerous animals. She lives in Columbus, Ohio, with her two hairless cats, who are not dangerous but look very strange.

www.rourkeeducationalmedia.com

PHOTO CREDITS: Cover, page 1: ©Holly Kuchera; pages 4-5: ©Ondrej Prosicky; pages 6-7: ©Andyworks; pages 8-9: ©DnDavis; pages 10-11, 30: ©Michal Ninger; pages 12-13: ©Chris de Billot; page 14 inset: ©danikancil; pages 14-15, 30: ©bendenhartog; pages 16-17, 30: ©Ondrej Prosicky; pages 18-19: ©undefined undefined; pages 20-21, 30: ©PaulReevesPhotography; pages 22-23, 30: chrisdorney; pages 24-25: ©JeffGoulden; pages 26-27, 30: ©JustinDutcher; page 28a: ©Dgwildlife; page 28b: ©BrianEKushner; page 29a: ©ca2hill; page 29b: ©Harlequin129; page 32: ©Taryn Lindsey

Edited by: Kim Thompson
Cover design by: Rhea Magaro-Wallace
Interior design by: Bobbie Houser

Library of Congress PCN Data

Vultures and Other Birds / Tracie Santos
 (Dangerous...or Not?)
 ISBN 978-1-73163-821-2 (hard cover)
 ISBN 978-1-73163-898-4 (soft cover)
 ISBN 978-1-73163-975-2 (e-Book)
 ISBN 978-1-73164-052-9 (e-Pub)
Library of Congress Control Number: 2020930251

Rourke Educational Media
Printed in the United States of America
01-1942011937